Sports Illustrated
FOOTBALL: OFFENSE

The Sports Illustrated Library

BOOKS ON TEAM SPORTS

Baseball
Basketball
Curling: Techniques
 and Strategy

Football: Defense
Football: Offense
Football: Quarterback

Ice Hockey
Pitching
Soccer
Volleyball

BOOKS ON INDIVIDUAL SPORTS

Fly Fishing
Golf
Handball
Horseback
 Riding

Skiing
Squash
Table Tennis

Tennis
Track: Running Events
Track: Field Events

BOOKS ON WATER SPORTS

Powerboating
Skin Diving and Snorkeling

Small Boat Sailing
Swimming and Diving

SPECIAL BOOKS

Dog Training
Safe Driving

Training with Weights

Sports Illustrated
FOOTBALL:
OFFENSE

By BUD WILKINSON

Illustrations by
Robert Handville

HARPER & ROW, PUBLISHERS, New York
Cambridge, Philadelphia, San Francisco,
London, Mexico City, São Paulo, Sydney

1817

U.S. Library of Congress Cataloging in Publication Data

Wilkinson, Charles Burnham.
  Sports illustrated football: offense.

  (Sports illustrated library)
  1. Football—Offense.   I. Handville, Robert Tompkins,
birth date   illus.   II. Sports illustrated (Chicago)
III. Title.
GV951.8.W5   796.33'22   72–2924
ISBN 0-06-015173-0
ISBN–0–397–00910–1 (pbk.)

Copyright © 1972 Time Inc.

82 83 84 85 86 15 14 13 12 11

Printed in the United States of America

Photographs from *Sports Illustrated*, © Time Inc.
Cover: Al Freni
Page 8: Lane Stewart
Pages 28 and 84: Walter Iooss, Jr.
Page 74: John Iacono
Page 94: Sheedy & Long

Contents

Sports Illustrated
FOOTBALL: OFFENSE

1

Introduction

FOOTBALL is a complex game that combines the essential elements of almost all popular participant sports: the speed of track, the throwing and catching of baseball and basketball, the body contact of wrestling and boxing, the kicking of soccer. In addition, the strategies and tactics can be as complex as those of chess and bridge. All these elements make football challenging for players and exciting for spectators.

The game can be divided into three basic phases—defensive football, the kicking game and offensive football. This book covers the offensive phase of the game, describing the basic techniques for the player or coach. Individual techniques of blocking and ball handling are the same regardless of the offensive formation being used. Thus, a player who masters these fundamentals can play effectively in any offensive system—the Open Set, the I Formation or the Wishbone.

The text is intended for the developing player, not the highly sophisticated, experienced athlete or coach. I won't attempt to examine in depth the arguments for and against various offensive systems and styles of play, for, although football is a complex game of infinite variety, the basics of the game are simple, and proper execution of the basics will ensure the success of the individual player as well as the team. The team that executes individual fundamentals best will win, providing they play together as a coordinated, highly motivated team.

However, from a coaching standpoint, the development of team morale is more difficult than it superficially appears to be. There are inherent contradictions between the individual ambitions of the players and their ability to contribute to the team. It is axiomatic that:

● Linemen prefer to play defense because they get more personal recognition by making tackles than by blocking on offense.

● Backs prefer to play offense because they get more recognition by being ball carriers than by being defensive players.

Nevertheless, each player must be willing to subordinate his personal goals for the good of the team if that team is to achieve its maximum potential.

2
The Balance of Offense and Defense

EVERY team game has a delicate balance between offense and defense; in football, it hinges on the use of the hands and arms. The rules give the defensive players almost unlimited use of their hands and arms, while offensive players may not use their forearms and hands in blocking. This restriction gives the defensive player a definite physical advantage.

Figure 1. Offensive Stance. The offensive player has a narrower area of contact and poorer balance.

Figure 2. Defensive Stance.
Full extension of the arms and hands gives the defensive player a wider area of contact and better balance.

To compensate, the offense *has the initiative*. With possession of the ball, they control the *timing* of the start of each play and the point of attack. Proper execution of the starting count enables the offense to get the jump on the defense. Knowing what play will be run enables the offensive team to be coordinated, with specific assignments for each player.

These two factors combine to offset the use of the hands and arms granted by the rules to the defense. The resulting balance gives equal potential for success to both the offense and the defense.

3

Conditioning

THE most common misconception concerning football is that it is mainly a game of size and strength. To a degree this is true, but it is also a game of speed and reaction. The physical demands of the various offensive positions enable men of a wide variety of physiques to play the game successfully. Slightly built men who have speed of foot and the ability to catch the ball can play effectively as wide receivers. Heavily built, slower types can be effective interior offensive linemen. Players of all-around ability are needed for the other positions.

A few generalizations about what type of offense to use:

• If the players are big and fast, it doesn't make much difference what formation you use.

• If the players are big and slow, you should use an assaulting type of offense, concentrating on straight-ahead, hard-hitting plays.

• If the players are small and fast, you should use a wide-open attack.

13

● If the players are small and slow, it won't make much difference since there's no way you'll be able to develop an effective attack.

With young players, care should be exercised to avoid physical mismatches. Boys bigger and stronger than others their age should play the interior line positions. If they are too superior physically, they should be moved up to a stronger arena of competition.

Football is a physical game; the team that hits hardest wins. However, leg strength and agility are more important than arm and shoulder strength, and since a team is only as good as its ability to move, young players should work on developing their legs. This can be accomplished by running and special exercises.

RUNNING EXERCISES

1. Jog. This loosens your muscles.
2. Sprint various distances. Five-yard bursts from a football stance (see page 18); then 10 and 20 yards.
3. Run sideways. To run to the left, keep the shoulders parallel to the direction of movement, cross the right leg over the left, then swing the left leg wide to the left and repeat for a distance of 20 yards. Run back in the opposite direction, crossing the left leg over the right.
4. Run backward. Reach back for the longest possible stride and raise the knees as high as possible while running backward for a distance of 20 yards.

SPECIAL EXERCISES

1. From a standing position raise one leg, grasp the shin and pull the knee and leg against the chest as high as possible. Repeat the exercise with the other leg.
2. Do the same exercise lying on your back.

14

3. Lie on your back, your arms extended at shoulder height on either side, and roll the right leg over and attempt to touch the left palm with the right toe. Roll to the left side and touch the right palm with the left toe.

4. In a standing position, cross your feet and, while keeping the knees straight, bend once from the waist and touch your fingertips or palms to the ground. If necessary, bob up and down to achieve maximum extension. Cross your feet the opposite way and repeat.

5. If a weight machine is available, develop greater strength in the legs by lifting weights with your feet. Instructions for doing this are available with the machine.

Players should warm up before beginning practice or play by jogging around the field and then doing a few or all of the exercises given above, or others the coach includes in his warm-up program.

PROTECTIVE EQUIPMENT

Adequate equipment is a must for participation in tackle football, and the first requirement is that it fit properly. If it hangs loose, it can be dangerous.

Minimum equipment includes a helmet, shoulder pads and football pants, which include hip pads, thigh pads and knee pads. Shoes should fit well, but football shoes are not a requirement. Tennis or basketball shoes, while not providing the best traction, are adequate for young players.

HITTING POSITION

All offensive and defensive contact in football is delivered from the same hitting position, which every football player must understand and practice until he can take the position shown in Figure 3 accurately at the moment of contact.

15

Figure 3. Hitting Position.
Bend your knees about 75 degrees; spread your feet apart about the width of your shoulders. Keep your back straight, your neck bulled. From this coiled position you can use the muscles of your legs, back, abdomen and shoulders to strike a hard blow, whether playing offense or defense.

USE OF EYES

Excellent vision is needed to play football effectively. However, it is useless if a football player closes his eyes just prior to contact. If he does, he is blind at the moment his opponent is trying his hardest to evade him. With eyes closed, he cannot see the evasive movement and consequently will miss his target. A quick blink at the moment of contact is inevitable, but constant practice and coaching can teach the player to avoid closing his eyes entirely.

4
Offensive Line Play

A

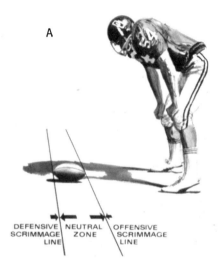

Figure 4.

A. The neutral zone is the length of the football. B. Offensive players, except the center, may not be ahead of their end of the ball. Defensive players may not be ahead of their end of the ball.

DEFENSIVE SCRIMMAGE LINE NEUTRAL ZONE OFFENSIVE SCRIMMAGE LINE

B

IT is a truism that the team that *controls the line of scrimmage* wins the game. Technically, prior to the snap of the ball, there are *two* lines of scrimmage separated by a neutral zone the length of the football, as shown in Figure 4A. Both teams can move when the ball is snapped. The offense can achieve control of the line of scrimmage by properly executing the starting count. This is made possible by flawless stances by all players and a coordinated explosive start by the offensive linemen.

THE STANCE

The four-point stance (Figure 5) is used by a few offensive football teams that do not require their linemen to pull out to lead wide plays. Oklahoma and Texas use this stance, since the Wishbone attack requires the linemen to charge straight ahead on almost all plays. However, on certain plays, most offensive teams require that their linemen pull to trap or pull to lead wide in addition to charging straight ahead to block. These linemen should use the three-point stance (Figure 6), and all linemen should learn it.

Figure 5. Four-Point Stance.

Squat, place both hands on the ground directly under the shoulders and drop one foot back so that the toe is parallel with the heel or instep of the other foot. Raise your hips until your back is parallel to the ground. Distribute your weight equally on your hands and feet, with enough weight forward to let you charge without having to make any preliminary movement or adjustment.

Figure 6. Three-Point Stance.
Squat and place your right hand on the ground directly ahead of your right knee, dropping your right foot back slightly. (Left-handed players use the left hand and foot.) Raise your hips to make your back parallel to the ground. Distribute your weight equally on the tripod formed by your feet and your hand.

Learn to step forward with either foot so that you can charge effectively to either side or straight ahead. Always step off with the foot closest to your opponent: if he's to the left, step off with the left foot, and vice versa.

In making a straight-ahead charge, your entire body must move forward with the snap of the ball. If your buttocks are raised too high, or if there is any other body movement before the charge, it will tip off the timing of the charge and you will lose the jump.

In pulling to trap, the offensive lineman takes the three-point stance. To trap to the left, push back with your hand as the ball is snapped and swing your left foot back about 18 inches as you turn your shoulders 45 degrees to the left, as shown in Figure 7. Then step toward the line of scrim-

Figure 7. Pulling to Trap to the Left.

mage on your right foot to maintain an inside angle on the player to be trapped. To trap to the right, take your first step with your right foot.

When pulling to lead a play wide, again assume the three-point stance. To lead to the left, push back with your hand as the ball is snapped and swing your left foot back about 10 inches and out about a foot, as in Figure 8. Then swing the right foot back and out away from the line of scrimmage past the left foot and circle around to position yourself for the block. When pulling to lead to the right, your right foot moves first.

Figure 8. Pulling to Lead to the Left.

BLOCKING TECHNIQUES

There are four basic blocks: the one-on-one shoulder block, the double-team block, the reach or scramble block and the open-field block—all designed to control the defense so that the backs can advance the ball. The secret of good blocking is to make and *maintain contact* with the opponent, and the blocker must have a definite target: the opponent's belt buckle.

20

The One-on-One Shoulder Block. To execute this block to the left, gauge your distance from the defensive player so that your shoulder hits on his belt buckle as your left foot hits the ground, as Figure 9 illustrates. Then step past him with your right foot. Follow through by taking shorter steps with your left foot than your right, thereby turning your opponent farther and farther to the left. When executing a shoulder block to the right, make contact with your right shoulder as your right foot hits the ground.

The position of the head is of *paramount* importance. Most poor blockers fail to bull their neck. Instead of holding their head directly over their shoulders, they tend to tilt it to the outside and look at the ground. They lose sight of the opponent and consequently miss the block. *Keep your head up, your neck bulled and your eyes on the target.*

Figure 9. The One-on-One Shoulder Block.

The Double-Team Block. This block is executed by two players, the "post" man and the "drive" man, working together in harmony. Figure 10 illustrates a double-team block to the left. First, the post man steps directly at the opponent with his right foot, aiming his right shoulder at the belt buckle and hitting with just enough force to neutralize the defensive player's charge and gain a standoff with him. At the same time the drive man steps directly at the opponent with his *left* foot, his target being the belt just inside the defensive player's left hip. He drives at this target with his left shoulder, bringing it into contact with his teammate's right shoulder, as seen in Figure 10. Then he steps with his right foot at a 45-degree angle past the hip of the defensive player. Both men then follow through with short, chopping steps—the post man pivoting on his left foot, the drive man taking shorter steps with his left foot than with his right to turn the opponent. The offensive players must keep their shoulders and hips together so that the defensive player cannot split between them.

Figure 10. The Double-Team Block.

The Reach or Scramble Block. This block is used to tie up an opponent who is playing outside the offensive man so that the play can be run around the defensive player. See Figure 11A. To scramble-block to the left, the blocker steps slightly back and out as far as possible with his left foot. He

Figure 11. The Reach or Scramble Block.

then steps laterally with his left foot and drives his right arm out past the defensive player (see 11B). As his right arm passes him, the blocker puts both hands on the ground (see 11C) and crawls on his hands and feet to turn his opponent back inside to the right.

The key to making a scramble block properly is to get the inside arm beyond the defensive player. Once this is done, leverage is obtained, making it possible to turn the player inside. In making this movement, the inside arm should be punched in an uppercut manner rather than in a sweeping hook. The uppercut ensures that the arm passes the opponent, whereas the hook motion does not.

The Pass Protection Block. This block is used to keep the backfield clear so that the quarterback can throw the ball. The offensive player moves from his stance to the hitting position and lets the opponent come to him. As the defender approaches the contact area, the blocker uncoils to break the charge, keeping his body in front of the defender to prevent him from penetrating into the backfield to the spot from which the quarterback will throw.

The Open-Field Block. This block is made against an opponent who has time and room to move to either side before the blocker reaches him. Again the key is: *Make and maintain contact with the defensive player.* Usually there is enough room for the ball carrier to get past the opponent to either side; therefore, the blocker should take his man the "easy" way: If the opponent is protecting to the left, take him left, and vice versa. The technique of making the block is either the same as for the shoulder block (see page 21) or the scramble block (see page 23).

THE TIGHT END

The tight end must be able to execute all of the blocking techniques of offensive guards and tackles. In addition, he should be a capable runner of pass routes and be able to catch the football. The routes he must be able to run and the technique of catching the ball are set forth in the next chapter on pass receiving.

THE CENTER

While the offensive guards and tackles need to be able to execute all of the blocks described above, the center has to be able to execute them while snapping the ball to the quarterback—a difficult task. The center's stance is the same as that of the other offensive linemen except that one hand must be grasping the ball in preparation for the snapback to the quarterback. Some centers put both hands on the ball, as in Figure 12A. Others cradle the free arm over the left knee (12B). Still others place the free hand on the ground since they feel it gives them better balance (12C).

Figure 12. The Center's Stance.

A

B

C

The center must charge as he snaps the ball. A common error is to snap the ball and then charge. But this permits the defensive player to hit and control the center prior to his charge. The snap can be executed best if the center assumes that he is lifting the ball and *charging over it* rather than snapping it back to the quarterback. As he charges, he must be able to execute the one-on-one block, the double-team block or the scramble block (see above). Very seldom do teams require the offensive center to trap or to lead wide.

The exchange between the center and the quarterback must be *automatic*. (For a discussion of this exchange, see pages 60–62.) The snap must be quick and clean. The center lifts the ball naturally into the hands of the quarterback. There must be no bobbing or fumbling.

5

Techniques of the Wide Receivers

THE most dramatic change in offensive football in recent years has been the development of the remarkable skills of the passers and receivers. Men like Lance Alworth, Bob Hayes, Gene Washington and the incomparable Paul Warfield, together with throwers like Unitas, Plunkett and Bob Griese, have revolutionized the game. By using an offensive formation with two wide receivers, the modern game forces the defense to cover the entire front from sideline to sideline as well as the total depth of the field from the line of scrimmage to the end line. The speed of foot, faking and double-faking of the wide receivers, plus their ability to catch the ball "in traffic," place immense and continuing pressure on the defense.

The wide receiver should take a stance like a sprinter,

but with only one hand on the ground. He should look to the inside to watch the center snap the ball. Because of his distance from the quarterback and the usual loud crowd noise, it might be hard for him to hear the snap count, so he must watch in order to be able to move as the ball is snapped.

While the wide receivers are primarily potential pass targets, they must also be able to block well in order to exploit their position to the fullest extent. It is comparatively easy for these men to get good blocking position, but the timing of the block is extremely difficult because they are so far ahead of the ball. When the ball carrier is only two steps behind the blocker, almost any contact by the blocker on the defensive player will make it easy for the ball carrier to get past the opponent. (See Open-Field Block, page 24.) However, if the block is made 10 yards or more ahead of the ball, even though the defensive player is knocked to the ground, he can often get up, recover and make the tackle. Thus, the wide receiver must time his block to hit the opponent when the ball carrier is close to him.

The two types of blocks made by the wide receiver are the pick-off block on a lineman or linebacker moving from the inside out to cover a wide play run to the side of the wide receiver and the downfield block after the receiver has faked running a deep pass route. Maintaining position on the defender is the key to making these two blocks successfully.

Wide receivers must learn to run accurate, elusive pass patterns. But, before running the pattern, the receiver has to *get off the line of scrimmage.* Defensive players will attempt to keep him from getting downfield by knocking him down at the line of scrimmage or shortly after he crosses it. Consequently, if the defense plays a man *on* the receiver *on* the line of scrimmage, the receiver has to be able to evade the man and get downfield.

Just prior to the snap of the ball, the receiver looks at all defensive players in his area. If a man is on or close to him, he should assume that this man will attempt to knock him down. As the ball is snapped, the receiver starts downfield, watching only the defensive player closest to him. The receiver can avoid him in a variety of ways. He can move quickly to his inside or his outside and then reverse direction to cut past the defender.

Or, if a defender is playing the receiver on the line of scrimmage, the receiver can take one step, make a sharp head fake to either side and then reverse direction to move past the defender. If the defender does not take the first fake, the receiver can go past him on the original course.

The rule here, as in all phases of the game, is to *use the eyes alertly*. If the receiver takes his eyes off his opponent, he will be knocked down because the defender will hit him when he is not looking. By seeing only the defender, and by faking properly as described above, the receiver will be able to get off the line of scrimmage past the defender and get into position to run his route to catch the ball.

Pass receivers run three different types of routes—individual patterns, in which the receiver attempts to get open by his own fakes; "combination" patterns, in which he and a teammate combine their patterns to enable the primary receiver to get open; and running "play action" passes, in which the fake of the running play entices the defensive secondary up to stop the run and thereby allows the receiver to get open.

INDIVIDUAL RUNNING PATTERNS

Different terms are used by different teams to describe individual patterns. However, in all cases they are basically descriptive of the patterns to be run.

The Slant Pattern. This pattern is designed to hit a receiver who is not being immediately covered by the defense. See Diagram 1. The receiver knows the ball will be thrown to him approximately one second after the ball has been snapped. The receiver moves at a 45-degree angle to the inside. He looks for the ball immediately. (The quarterback should not allow this play to be run if a defender is playing in position to cut off the slant pattern. When this occurs, the quarterback should check signals at the line of scrimmage to another play.)

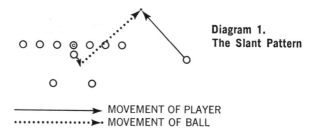

**Diagram 1.
The Slant Pattern**

⟶ MOVEMENT OF PLAYER
•••••••••► MOVEMENT OF BALL

The Hitch Pattern. This pattern should be used when the defender is playing deep off the line of scrimmage, fearing the receiver will have enough speed to get behind him. The receiver takes two steps downfield, then drops back a step while looking for the ball. See Diagram 2. If the defender is playing on the line of scrimmage or within a yard or two of the receiver, the quarterback should check signals.

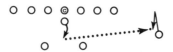

**Diagram 2.
The Hitch Pattern**

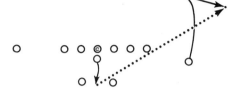

Diagram 3.
The Sideline Pattern

The Sideline Pattern. On this pattern the receiver breaks down the field as fast as possible and attempts to lure the defender into turning and running to keep the receiver from getting behind him. As the defender turns to run, the receiver plants his inside foot and breaks on a slight angle back and toward the sideline. See Diagram 3.

The exact timing of the cut when used on the last available down will depend on the yardage needed on the play. For example, when the ball is on your 35-yard line on third down and you need 6 yards to make the first down, the receiver should break to go out of bounds at about 7 yards from the line of scrimmage. If 12 yards are needed, the receiver should make his break to go out of bounds approximately 13 yards from the line of scrimmage.

The passer and receiver must practice the timing on the various depths of the cut so that the ball will be thrown just as the receiver plants his foot to begin his break to the outside. If the passer waits until the receiver has made his break, the receiver may run out of bounds before the ball reaches him.

It is of paramount importance for the passer to throw the ball on a line only chest high at the receiver. This will enable the receiver to keep his torso and shoulders between the defender and the ball to protect it from the opponent as the catch is made and eliminate any chance of an interception.

33

The Curl or Hook Pattern. Here, the receiver goes off the line of scrimmage exactly as he does on the sideline cut. He drives downfield as fast as possible while keeping his body under control. He should drive for a spot about 2 yards outside the man covering him. This will force the defender to move to the outside. As the defender moves back and to the outside, the receiver curls to the inside, getting his back and shoulders between the defender and the flight of the ball. See Diagram 4. The curl should be made at the distance necessary to gain needed yardage on the play, as explained for the sideline cut on page 33. Again, the ball should be delivered at the receiver at chest height.

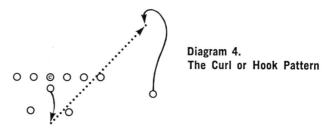

Diagram 4.
The Curl or Hook Pattern

The Flag Pattern. On this pattern the receiver attempts to get behind the defender. He moves off the line of scrimmage in the normal manner, floats at about three-quarter speed while watching the defender, then breaks full speed for the flag at the goal line on the sideline. See Diagram 5. The receiver should not look for the ball until he is past the defender. This timing must be carefully worked out in practice. The ball will be put in the air about 3 to 4 seconds after it is snapped. The receiver should not look for the ball until it has been thrown.

Diagram 5.
The Flag Pattern

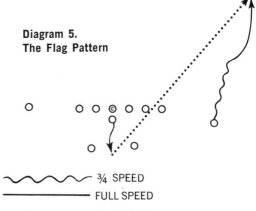

~~~~~ ¾ SPEED
————— FULL SPEED

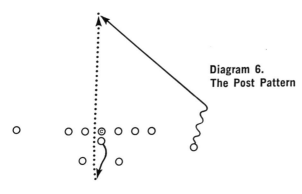

**Diagram 6.
The Post Pattern**

The Post Pattern. In running this route, the receiver again comes off the line of scrimmage normally, floats as he did on the flag pattern and then turns on the speed, running at an angle that will put him directly in the middle of the goalposts on the end line. See Diagram 6. He should not look for the ball until it is thrown, which will be approximately 3 to 4 seconds after the ball is snapped.

The Sideline–Flag Pattern. When the receiver is being covered closely by the defender on the sideline pattern, it is comparatively simple to get behind the defender by faking the sideline pattern and going deep (assuming the passer can be protected long enough). The receiver runs the sideline pattern exactly as described on page 33. After making the break, he takes eight or ten steps on the sideline cut, being certain to keep his body under perfect control. He then plants his outside foot and turns downfield, utilizing his full speed to run the flag pattern past the defender. See Diagram 7.

Diagram 7. The Sideline–Flag Pattern. Quarterback fakes a throw and then, when the receiver breaks to the sideline, he resets and throws deep.

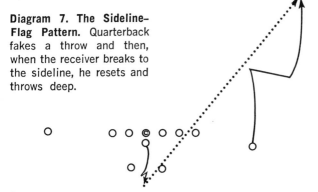

Diagram 8. The Sideline–Flag–Sideline Pattern. Quarterback fakes a throw and then, when the receiver breaks to the sideline, he resets and throws deep.

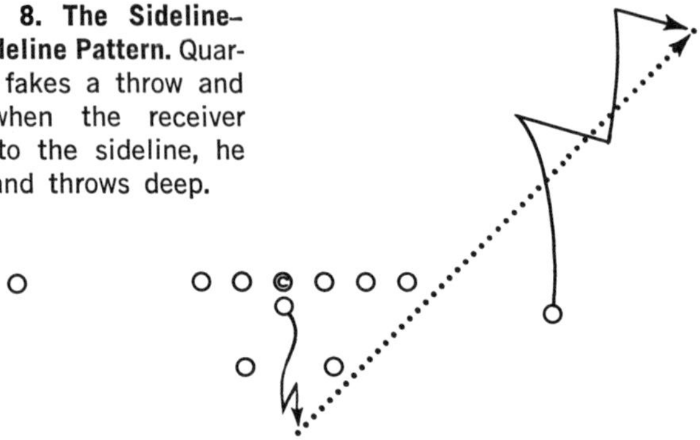

The Sideline–Flag–Sideline Pattern. Here, the receiver combines the sideline–flag pattern with a second sideline cut. He runs the sideline pattern, breaks downfield and then, after moving 6 to 8 yards, he again plants the inside foot and runs a second sideline cut. See Diagram 8. It is almost impossible for the defender to cover this pattern. But since it takes a relatively long time to run the pattern properly, the pass protection must be exceptionally good if the passer is to have time to throw the ball.

The Curl–Sideline Pattern. On this pattern the receiver runs the curl pattern as described on page 34. Having made the curl to the inside, he plants his inside foot and breaks on a sideline pattern to the outside. See Diagram 9.

Diagram 9. The Curl–Sideline Pattern. Quarterback fakes a throw and then, when the receiver breaks to the sideline, he resets and throws deep.

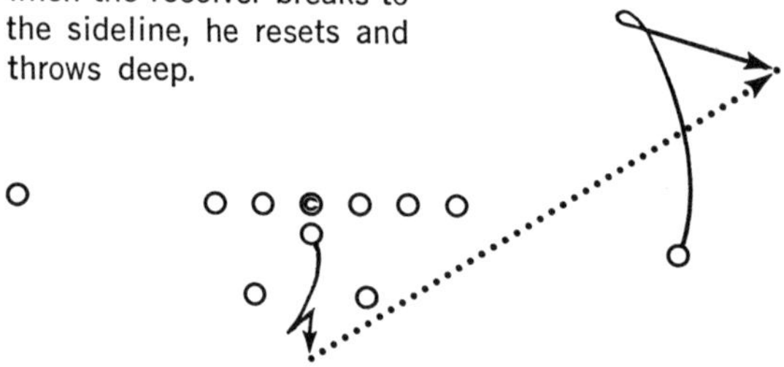

Actually, there is an almost infinite variety of routes which can be adapted from the basic patterns just described. The pattern to be run would be descriptive of the continuing breaks to be made by the receiver.

COMBINATION PATTERNS

Combination patterns between two receivers to open one man are also designated by self-descriptive terms: "flanker–flag" "tight–end–out" (Diagram 10), "split–end–curl" "half-back–flag" (Diagram 11) and "ends–cross" (Diagram 12). There are many other patterns, and the following three diagrams illustrate the theory.

Diagram 10. "Flanker–Flag" "Tight–End–Out"   Pattern. The flanker runs the flag route (Diagram 5, page 34) to take the defensive man back deep and thus clear the flat area for the tight end who will break to the flat about four yards deep.

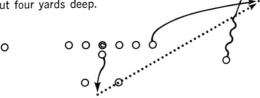

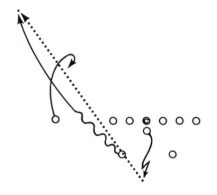

Diagram 11. "Split–End–Curl" "Halfback–Flag" Pattern. The split end runs his regular curl route (Diagram 4, page 34). As he makes the curl, the quarterback pumps and fakes a throw to him to draw the defensive halfback up to cover the curl. The halfback floats out of the backfield, running low to conceal, if possible, his movement from the defense. As the end curls, he breaks full speed deep on the flag route, attempting to get behind the defensive halfback. The quarterback resets and throws deep to the offensive halfback.

Diagram 12. "Ends–Cross" Pattern. The split end drives at the outside leg of the defensive halfback to widen him slightly. Eight yards from the line of scrimmage, he breaks straight down the field to take his opponent deep. The tight end clears the line of scrimmage and watches the defensive halfback on the far side. As that man moves back to cover the split end, the offensive tight end breaks full speed for the open area in front of the defensive halfback.

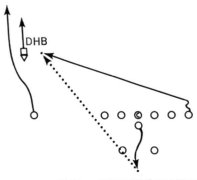

DHB — DEFENSIVE HALFBACK

PLAY ACTION PASSES

Getting the receiver open on a play action pass depends on the ball handling and faking of the quarterback and the running back.

It is possible to run an effective pass play from almost every running play. This tactic helps the running attack, since the defensive secondary cannot support against the run until they are *positive* the play is *not* a pass. The following is one example.

The Toss-Trap Pass. As the ball is snapped, the quarterback fakes a quick toss to the flaring halfback and then makes a careful perfect fake to the halfback hitting in on the inside play. After completing the fake (see page 63) he moves slowly back to his passing position. Meanwhile the tight end moves downfield on a sharp inside angle as if he were positioning himself to block the safety man on the trap. As the safety moves up to stop the faked trap, the end breaks past him on the post pattern. See Diagram 13.

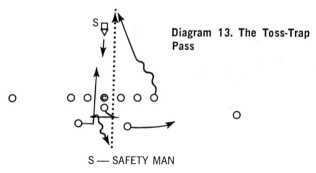

Diagram 13. The Toss-Trap Pass

S — SAFETY MAN

HOW TO CATCH THE BALL

Catching the ball requires disciplined use of the hands and eyes. Two common errors prevent players from becoming capable receivers:

(1). Looking for the ball too soon. Until the ball is in

the air (depending on the play), the receiver may be considered a potential blocker, and defenders are at liberty to hit him and knock him down. To avoid this, the receiver should watch the movements of the defensive players in his area and not turn to look for the ball until he knows the quarterback is ready for release.

Different pass plays have a variety of timings of delivery of the ball. The longer the ball is in the air, the longer the

Figure 13. "Looking the Ball Into the Hands."

A. Wrong

receiver can delay in looking for it. The quarterback and the receiver should practice together on "count passes." For instance, the quarterback may deliver the ball at the count of five. The receiver goes down the field, making whatever fakes fit the pass route to be run, makes the final break at the count of five and then turns to look for the ball, knowing that it will be on its way.

(2). Taking his eyes off the ball just before it reaches him. (See Figure 13.) The receiver's failure to "look the

B. Right

ball into the hands" can cause the pass to be missed. The temptation to take his eyes off the ball is real and understandable since he sees the ball on its way and knows he can make the catch. Instinctively he wants to look at possible defenders who may be closing on him to make the tackle. But if he takes his eyes off the ball he won't be able to make the catch because he has broken the hand–eye coordination necessary to properly receive the ball.

The hands must be in a soft, relaxed position at the time the catch is made, as shown in Figure 14B. The receiver should run his pass route, using his hands and arms to lend balance and give additional speed to his running, not raising them to catch the ball until it is close to the receiver,

Figure 14.

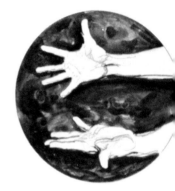

A. Wrong

B. Right

as Figure 15B illustrates. Reaching for the ball too soon gets the receiver off balance, tensing the hands and arms and making the catch more difficult.

Figure 15.

A. Wrong

B. Right

Drills. Here are two drills that quickly improve the ability of pass receivers:

(1). To learn hand softness, the receiver should be about 3 yards to the left of the coach, who will toss the ball to him. He runs half-speed straight ahead. The ball is tossed softly a distance of about 8 to 10 yards. The receiver catches the ball one-handed with his left hand. Repeat the drill with the coach tossing the ball from about 3 yards to the receiver's left so that he catches the ball one-handed with the right hand. He will quickly learn the proper hand softness needed to cradle the ball as it is caught. It also helps to develop good hand-eye coordination, since he must watch the ball carefully to catch and hold it with one hand.

(2). To help teach the receiver to see the ball into his hands, write numerals in chalk or ink on both ends of the ball on each of its four panels (see Figure 16) and ask him to run the regular pass patterns and call out the number on the ball at the moment he catches it.

Figure 16.

44

6
Play of the Running Backs

THE skill of the running backs determines the potential of the offensive team's running attack. The essential physical talents are speed, balance, agility and the ability to change direction.

The mental requirements are equally important. The running back is a major target. Defensive players use all their physical toughness in an attempt to intimidate him, so the running back must have a total commitment to scoring a touchdown each time he is given the ball. With this commitment, he will always fight for extra yardage by making a determined second, third and fourth effort to stay on his feet and move toward the goal rather than surrender to the first tackler who gets to him.

BLOCKING

The effectiveness of his teammates' blocking skill is the major determinant of the running back's opportunity to make yardage. But the running back must also possess blocking ability. By blocking well for the other backs, he improves his team's morale tremendously. If he is a prima donna and does not block effectively, a deterioration in team attitude takes place, and over a period of time the other offensive players will not block for him as well as they could. For this reason it is essential that every running back sharpen his own blocking capability so that his teammates will respect him as a football player.

Running backs need to execute four types of blocks: blocking a man out, blocking a man in, taking a man either way with an "isolation" block, and blocking to protect the passer. The key to all blocks is: *Get the proper position on the opponent; and maintain contact.*

Blocking An Opponent Out. To effectively block the opponent out, the back must get his *inside foot* closer to the line of scrimmage than the opponent's. Once he's in this position (see Figure 17), the block becomes simply the regular shoulder block described on page 21. The back

Figure 17. Blocking an Opponent Out.

should expect the defender to make the toughest possible charge as the ball is snapped—which means to come down the line of scrimmage from the outside to the inside without getting any depth across the line of scrimmage. So, when the ball is snapped, the back moves at such an angle that he can meet his opponent at the "crossroads" and still have his inside foot closer to the line of scrimmage than the defensive man's. As he moves, he should intently watch his opponent. If the man makes a normal charge across the line of scrimmage slightly to the inside, the blocking back can adjust his course as soon as he has gained inside-out position. As he reaches the area of impact, he should have a good base, be in the hitting position and deliver the block with a sharp thrust of the back, shoulders and legs. The target remains the same—the opponent's belt buckle.

Blocking An Opponent In. The hook-in block is much like the scramble block described for linemen (page 23). Again, the back expects the defender to move on a course that will make the block as difficult as possible. This would be to

Figure 18. Blocking an Opponent In.

come softly straight across the line of scrimmage ready to give ground to the outside. To make the play, the blocker must get his outside foot *beyond* the outside foot of the defender, as shown in Figure 18.

To block a man in while moving to the right, the blocker moves straight for the sidelines from his original position, watching his opponent. He *must* remain deeper than the opponent (see next paragraph). If the opponent crosses the line rapidly and is approaching a point deeper than the blocker, the blocker must give ground to remain deeper than the defender. As the blocker approaches the area of contact, he should be in the hitting position. He must stay on his feet and get his right foot farther to the outside than either foot of the defender. As this position is reached, he swings his left arm with the upper-cut motion, getting the elbow and upper arm beyond the thigh and hip of the opponent. He then follows through with his left thigh hooking the opponent by driving off the right leg.

If the defensive man is determined to get deeper across the line of scrimmage than the blocker, the blocker should let him get a yard deeper and position himself for the regular hook-in block. But then, driving off his right foot, he should swing his hips and legs to the right and make a "reverse body block," knocking the opponent out. The block will be made so deep across the line of scrimmage that the ball carrier can run his regular course even though he goes inside the defensive man.

As the ball is snapped, the blocker must watch the opponent. If he does not make the difficult charge but instead moves to the inside and does not attempt to get much depth into the backfield, the blocker will adjust his course to put himself in position to execute the block as described.

Hooking a man in while moving to the left is done exactly the same way except that the left foot must be outside the defender at the moment the block is made.

The Isolation Block. The isolation block is used against a lineman or linebacker left exposed by double-team blocks of the linemen which usually open a big hole at the line of scrimmage. The mission of the back is to take on his opponent squarely and let the ball carrier run for daylight to either side of the block. Again, the essential is to make and *keep contact.*

As the ball is snapped, the blocker moves directly at his opponent, keeping his eyes squarely on the belt buckle. As he approaches the area of contact, he should be in a low hitting position and have enough momentum to meet and if possible overpower the defender. The defender cannot protect both sides against the blocker. If the blocker is moving with force and intensity, the defender must go around the blocker to get at the ball carrier. As he commits himself, the blocker adjusts to hit with the proper shoulder to make and keep contact. The ball carrier watches the defensive player and adjusts his course to go to the side opposite the move of the defender.

The Pass Protection Block. The pass protection block is essentially one of defending an area. The blocker knows where the quarterback will set up to throw, and his purpose is to keep the defensive man from penetrating to that spot. Since the defensive pass rushers will use a variety of patterns, the blocker does not know which man he will block until a defensive player arrives in his area.

As the ball is snapped, the blocker moves to the spot where he will protect the quarterback. As pass rushers move toward him, he watches intently to pick the man coming into his area. He makes the block by hitting with his outside shoulder to turn the defender out around the quarterback. Again, he makes and *maintains contact* as he rolls his man to the outside.

If the rusher flattens his charge so that the blocker cannot hit him with his outside shoulder, the blocker must have enough balance to hit with the inside shoulder, turn the defender to the inside and take him past the throwing lane.

49

RECEIVING THE BALL

The ball carrier gets the ball one of two ways: a hand-off from the quarterback or a toss from the quarterback. On the hand-off, the running back is moving with maximum speed and the quarterback must delicately place the ball on the back's outside hip. The quarterback should think of the ball

Figure 19. Receiving the Ball.

A. Right

50

as being a hollow eggshell, softly handing it to the running back instead of slapping it against the hip.

The hand and arm position when receiving the hand-off is of vital importance. The outside hand should be curled in slightly just inside the hip to block the ball if the quarterback extends it too far. The inside elbow should be up, with the forearm parallel to the ground, opening the target (the outside hip) for the quarterback. See Figure 19A. In Figure 19B, the inside elbow is too low, blocking the ball.

B. Wrong

Figure 20. The receiver takes the hand-off while watching the defensive players in the area he will hit.

A good ball carrier takes the hand-off from feel, watching only the defensive players in the area he will hit. If he looks for the ball, he'll lose sight of the defense and miss the holes. By keeping his eyes focused on the area to be attacked, he can react to the movements of the defensive players and cut accordingly.

When the ball carrier feels the ball being placed on his far hip (see Figure 20) he drops his inside elbow over the ball and cradles it with both hands and arms. Dropping his inside elbow over the ball protects it if he is hit during the hand-off. If the blocking is effective and he breaks past the line of scrimmage, he can grasp the ball with either hand and move it to the proper carrying position.

When the ball is tossed to the running back on a pitchout, he must "look it into his hands" while running as fast as possible. Just as in pass receiving, taking the eyes off the ball is disastrous.

Fumbles—devastating in their effect on the offense—will not occur if the quarterback and ball carriers painstakingly practice hand-offs and pitchouts.

Also, the ball must be carried properly. One point of the ball should rest in the palm of the ball carrier's hand with the opposite end tucked underneath the elbow, as shown in Figure 21. This protects both points of the ball, preventing a tackler from hooking it away, causing a fumble. A common mistake is to expose the point of the ball by having the thumb and forefinger wrapped around the end of the ball rather than protecting the point with the palm of the hand.

In open-field running, the hand and arm carrying the ball can be moved away from the body to aid the carrier's balance and thus his speed. However, if he is in imminent danger of being tackled, he should bring the ball in tight against the rib cage to protect it.

Figure 21. Proper Ball-carrying Position.

The ability to run for daylight is the running back's most important skill. Great runners like Gale Sayers, Duane Thomas, Matt Snell and O. J. Simpson are not necessarily built alike, but they possess the uncanny ability to watch and read the defense, find the hole and accelerate through it.

All great ball carriers have the ability to accelerate beyond their normal running speed. Gale Sayers is an outstanding example. Apparently running full speed, he has an additional burst of speed in reserve. This extra speed is the quality that separates the great from the ordinary runners.

WATCHING THE DEFENSIVE MAN

Coaches debate whether it is better for the running back to watch his own blockers or to watch the defensive men. While watching the blockers seems logical, it is actually much better to watch the defensive man. The blocker will be attempting to knock him to one side or the other. If the runner expects the block to be successful but the defensive player beats the blocker, he will be tackled. However, if he watches *the defensive man,* he will always be able to break to the proper side, as Figure 22 illustrates. Thus it is essential that the receiver *watch the defensive man rather than his own blocker.*

FAKING WITHOUT THE BALL

The most difficult fundamental for the running back to execute consistently well is to *fake carrying the ball.* It is axiomatic that if the defense believes the man has the ball, they'll go all out to hit him. If the faking back immediately shows the defense that he doesn't have the ball, he won't be hit nearly as hard. And since it is instinctive to avoid being hit, faking consistently well requires intensity of purpose. See Figure 23.

Figure 22.

A. The receiver watches the defensive man to see which side he will protect.

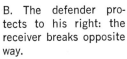

B. The defender protects to his right: the receiver breaks opposite way.

C. The defender protects to his left: the receiver breaks to the right.

The runner should curl to the inside upfield to hide the quarterback from the defense. By grasping both elbows with both hands, he will appear to have the ball. Using the same elusiveness as he would if he had the ball, he should continue running until tackled.

Figure 23.

A. In faking to get the ball, the runner puts his hands and arms in the same position as he would to get the ball in a hand-off, and the quarterback puts the ball into the far hip.

B. The runner drops his inside elbow as if to cover the ball as the quarterback pulls it back out. The player then fakes running with the ball.

RUNNING WITH THE BALL

Speed and power are obviously basic attributes of the ball carrier. Mercury Morris can run away from you; Jim Nance can run over you. But shiftiness is important too. Once past the line of scrimmage, the ball carrier should use all his speed and elusiveness to evade tacklers. Techniques can be taught, such as the stiff arm, the cross-over step and the fade-away step. However, most great ball carriers have natural reflexes that are largely unteachable to the less talented. Hall of Famer Hugh McIlhenny, when past his prime, once brought two outstanding defense men to their knees with head and shoulder fakes, first to one side, then the other, and ran between them for a touchdown.

7
The Quarterback

THE quarterback is the key player on the offensive team. Since he initiates every play, his skill is basic to the success of every play. The quarterback's duties are twofold: He must execute each play with mechanical perfection and, in addition, must lead the team and set the offensive strategy by his play selection. Many coaches eliminate the second responsibility of the quarterback (strategy and play selection) by calling all plays from the sidelines.

Being relieved of play-calling enables the quarterback to concentrate totally on mechanical execution. However, when a play is called from the sidelines by a coach, a particular defensive alignment is assumed. If the defense uses a different pattern, it may be strong against the play called. At this point the quarterback should check signals to change the play. If he is capable of doing this and calling a play that avoids running against that strong alignment, he is in all likelihood capable of total play selection without help from the sidelines.

THE STARTING COUNT

The offensive play actually begins when the quarterback enters the huddle. He *should not* enter until the rest of the players are in position. By waiting, he avoids the possibility of getting bad advice from his teammates. While the huddle forms, he should ascertain the down and yardage situation and the lateral and vertical field position of the ball and decide on the next play. He then joins the huddle and takes command of the team. He calls the formation, play and snap count with confidence, his voice and bearing completely dominating and controlling his men.

Having called the signals, the quarterback commands, "Break," the team moves to the line of scrimmage and sets up in the formation called. The quarterback positions himself behind the center, ready for the snap. He analyzes the defense to be certain that the play called has a reasonable chance of success. If not, he should check signals.

The quarterback's voice must be loud and clear when he calls the starting count or checks signals, since the team *must hear the signals* if they are to respond properly. The quarterback should call the snap count in a staccato tone so that the players develop a rhythm and break together to attack. (See page 85 for a starting count drill.)

As the starting count is called, the center snaps the ball to the quarterback. The quarterback's hands are placed under the center's crotch, turned about 30 degrees to the left. The thumbs of the hands are together, the fingers are spread naturally with the right forefinger in the middle of the center's crotch, touching with enough pressure so that the center can clearly feel the location of the quarterback's hands, which must remain in that position in the crotch until the ball actually reaches them.

The normal rotation of the ball as the center's arm and hand swing up and back will place the laces of the ball across the fingers of the quarterback's throwing hand. This gives him the "fat" of the ball and enables him to throw or

Figure 24.

A. Proper Exchange

B. Poor Exchange

hand the ball to another back without rotating it. See Figure 25.

The center and the quarterback should practice constantly until the exchange becomes automatic. The hand-back must be executed as fast as possible and be absolutely foolproof. *No fumbles!*

Figure 25. The quarterback grasps the ball with his fingers over the laces to give him the proper "feel" and control of the ball.

THE HAND-OFF

In making a hand-off, the quarterback knows which back will get the ball at what point in the backfield. As soon as he has the ball, his eyes should focus on the far hip of his receiver. Concentration on this small target requires discipline. The tendency of an inexperienced quarterback is to be overly aware of the defense and see the running back only as a somewhat blurred object. By focusing on the proper small target, he will be able to place the ball delicately on the far hip. If he can't reach that hip, he should keep the ball to avoid a fumble. Ironically, when the quarterback does miss the hand-off and keeps the ball, the play usually is successful because the running back expects to get the ball and will make an excellent fake since he will be running with maximum power in the expectation of being the ball carrier.

After handing the ball off, the quarterback must *never* let his eyes follow the ball carrier. Instead, he should carry out the continuing play fake.

FAKING A HAND-OFF

In faking the hand-off, the proper use of the quarterback's eyes to mislead the defense is essential. All of us are curious by nature. We tend to look at whatever anyone else is staring at. Similarly, the defense will tend to commit itself toward whatever back the quarterback looks at.

When he is actually going to hand the ball off, the quarterback must move to the ball carrier. When the quarterback is to fake giving the ball, the ball carrier must come to the quarterback.

When faking the hand-off, the quarterback should hold the fat of the ball in both hands, quickly reaching out

Figure 26. Quarterback Faking and Keeping the Ball.

with it to hit the stomach of the faking back and then riding the ball with the faking back as he hits toward the line of scrimmage (see page 56). As the back clears the quarterback, the quarterback should pull the ball back and place it on his own hip while following the faking back with an empty hand and a hard stare as shown in Figure 26. This must be done in a firm, confident manner so that the defense believes that the faking back has the ball. The quarterback must not rush his next move: He should give the defense ample time to take the fake.

THE QUARTERBACK OPTION PLAY

The quarterback option is the most significant offensive development in college football in the past few years. In its pure form the quarterback simply runs at the defensive

Figure 27. **Quarterback Option Play:** He passes.

A

end with a trailing back approximately 5 yards deeper than the quarterback. If the end moves in to tackle the quarterback, the quarterback tosses the ball back to the trailing halfback. See Figure 27. If the end crosses the line deep to protect against the possible pitch, the quarterback keeps the ball and turns upfield. See Figure 28. The play is easy to execute if the quarterback will do one thing: *Watch the defensive end.* Whatever the end does will be wrong.

The quarterback holds the ball approximately chest high, balancing it in both hands but controlling it with the right hand when moving to the right; with the left hand when moving to the left. He should move at the end with as much speed as possible while still maintaining the balance necessary to make a right-angle turn upfield if the end crosses the line to protect against the pitch.

As the quarterback angles toward the line of scrimmage, he should be sure to gain ground. By doing this, he pressures

Figure 28. Quarterback Option Play: He keeps the ball.

the defensive end to commit himself to stopping him or letting him keep the ball. While moving on this course the quarterback intently watches the end, ready to play it either way, depending on the movement of the end. If the end gets deeper than he is, the quarterback immediately plants his outside foot and turns upfield to run for daylight. If the end stays on the line of scrimmage and moves toward him, the quarterback simply flips the ball with the control hand in a soft, high pass to the trailing back.

The pass should be thrown shoulder high so that the trailing back can catch it easily while running full speed without losing momentum. A low pitch may cause him to

B

stumble or fumble, or slow him up by having to bend over in order to make the catch.

When the quarterback keeps the ball, he must operate as effectively as possible as a ball carrier. The fundamentals involved here were discussed in Chapter 6 on the running backs, pages 45–58.

THE FORWARD PASS

In modern offensive football the quarterback must be able

to throw forward passes consistently well. The defense is pressured by not knowing whether the play will be a pass or a run. If the quarterback is *not* a skillful passer, the defense is able to gamble that he will not be able to complete the pass even though the receiver is open. By ignoring the pass possibility, they can be effective against the running attack. Let me repeat: *The quarterback must be able to throw consistently and accurately.*

He should be able to throw both from a standing set position for drop-back passes and on the run. The running pass puts great pressure on the defense. If they drop back to cover the pass, the quarterback can run with the ball. If the defense commits to stop the threatened run, he can throw the ball to an open receiver.

The Drop-Back Pass. Since it is easier to throw the ball from the set position, the majority of coaches base their pass attack on the drop-back pass. To execute it, the quarterback has to move to the passing position as quickly as possible after the snap from center. This can be done in two ways. If the quarterback is a gifted athlete, he can drop straight back, thus facing the line of scrimmage and watching the movement of the defense the whole time. If he can't run backward fast enough without losing balance, it may be necessary for him to turn and run back to the set position while looking over his shoulder at the defensive team.

The depth to which the quarterback drops back varies depending on the play: The longer the pass, the deeper the drop; the sooner the pass is to be thrown, the shorter the drop. Once in position, the quarterback should look at the *defensive man* covering the primary receiver. If he is in position to cover, the quarterback should look for his secondary receiver or throw the ball away (by throwing it out of bounds or beyond everyone).

The quarterback *should not look* at his primary receiver (he knows where *he* will go). By looking only at the receiver, he will not be conscious of the defensive man and

A

B

C

Figure 29. The Drop-back Pass.

an interception may result. By watching the key defensive man, the quarterback sharply reduces the chances of an interception.

In preparing to pass, he should have the ball in both hands approximately shoulder high. When ready to throw, he steps forward with his left foot (assuming he is right-handed), stepping directly on the line he will throw the ball, and cocks the ball behind his right ear, holding it with his fingers across the laces, as Figure 29A illustrates. In delivering the ball, he lets it rotate off the palm of his hands to the fingertips in order to give it a spiral motion, as shown in 29B. He then follows through in the same manner as a baseball pitcher does. After the ball is released, his throwing hand should be shoulder high with the palm facing the ground, as in 29C.

The quarterback should learn to throw two types of passes: a fast clothes-line, high driving pass and a lofted soft ball.

The line-drive pass should be used to hit in front of the secondary defenders when the receiver has run such patterns as the slant, the sideline and the curl. The ball must *not* remain in the air long enough to let the defense get to it before it reaches the receiver.

The lofted pass should be used on deep cuts (the receiver will be attempting to get behind all defensive men) and must be lofted over the defensive men to the receiver.

The Running Pass. The actual delivery of the ball on the running pass is performed in the same way as on the drop-back pass. However, since the thrower will be running at practically full speed, additional techniques must be learned.

The right-handed passer will not have too much trouble throwing the ball while moving to his right. But when moving to his left (see Figure 30), he must twist his upper body against the momentum of his run, which makes it virtually impossible to throw the ball hard or with accuracy. (The reverse is true for the left-handed passer.)

Figure 30. The Running Pass: Throwing against the momentum of the body.

The key to throwing well on the run is to be moving *toward the line of scrimmage* at the time the ball is delivered. By doing this, the passer's momentum aids the delivery of the ball. (See Figure 31.) Again, the passer should read *the defensive man* covering the primary receiver instead of looking at the receiver.

Figure 31. The Running Pass. Turning upfield to throw the ball.

A

B

8

Basic Offensive Formations

THE major change in offensive formations in recent years has been the increased use of wide receivers—flankers and split ends—which forces the defense to cover the field from sideline to sideline on every snap. When teams use a compact formation like the Single Wing or the straight T, the defense can surround the formation reasonably well, since it covers only about 45 feet of the 160-foot width of the field. Consistent passing from the compact sets is difficult because all the receivers are close together when the ball is snapped. With detached men, all possible receivers are already separated by great distances, putting additional pressure on the defensive team.

It should be noted, however, that unless the offensive team has a strong-armed quarterback who can deliver the ball accurately with reasonable range, it is a waste of time, and poor strategy, to detach receivers. The defense can ignore them since the quarterback will not be able to get the ball to them anyway.

The need to spread the defense has resulted in almost all teams playing with at least one detached receiver, and the vast majority of teams use two. The free substitution rule has made it possible to play men as receivers who possess tremendous speed but who may not have the physical qualities required for other positions. They learn to run routes with great deception because they devote almost all of their practice time to perfecting their receiving skills.

On all formations the interior line plays exactly the same. The center, guards and tackles take their positions with no variations except a slight adjustment in the distances between offensive linemen. (The Split-T attack is based on changing the splits between linemen.) The major formation changes result from the placement of the offensive backs and ends.

THE OPEN SET

Popularized by the professional teams, the open formation consists of a split end and a flankerback, with one tight end and two running backs. The running backs usually take their position about 4 yards behind the offensive tackles, but their positions vary depending on the play. The Open Set has these advantages:

(1). It is perfectly balanced to either side.

(2). It makes the pass play a constant threat since there is a wide receiver out to each side.

(3). It provides for balanced running since either running back can hit quickly straight ahead or off tackle.

The major weakness of the Open Set is its inability to generate power inside. With only two running backs in the formation, it is difficult to hit quickly and still have a back leading inside plays.

76

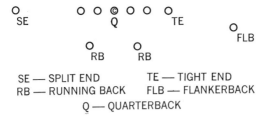

SE — SPLIT END   TE — TIGHT END
RB — RUNNING BACK   FLB — FLANKERBACK
Q — QUARTERBACK

Diagram 14. The Open Set

The Open Set is easily adjusted to put additional pressure on the defensive team. The common adjustments are the Twin Set and the Spread Set.

THE TWIN SET

Both wide receivers are on the same side of the field opposite the tight end. This pattern pressures the defense because the two most effective receivers can now closely coordinate their pass routes and use each other to free one man.

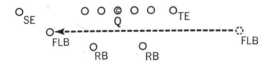

Diagram 15. The Twin Set. Both wide receivers to the same side.

THE SPREAD SET

Either one or both running backs are moved out of the backfield. This adjustment puts four or five receivers spread out across the field and pressures the defense to cover all men with the snap of the ball. (See Diagram 16 on page 78.)

However, moving the backs out reduces the team's ability to run effectively. If one back is moved out, the defense knows that, if the play is a run, either the quarterback or

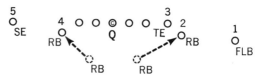

Diagram 16. The Spread Set. One or both running backs are moved up. This formation has 4 or 5 quick receivers.

the remaining back will carry the ball. If both are moved out, only the quarterback remains as a running threat.

THE I FORMATION

This formation is exactly the same as the Open Set except that the running backs are positioned differently. The fullback is in a three-point stance about 3½ yards from the line of scrimmage. The tailback stands erect about 5½ yards from the line of scrimmage so that he can see the defense over his fullback all of the time.

This formation generates a powerful inside running attack since the fullback is in position to lead the tailback on running plays. The formation gains additional strength from the quickness with which the fullback can hit inside. It retains the same passing strength as the Open Set.

Diagram 17. The I Formation. The running backs become fullback and tailback.

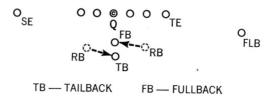

TB — TAILBACK   FB — FULLBACK

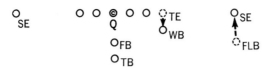

WB — WINGBACK

Diagram 18. The I Slot. The tight end drops back to become wingback; The flankerback moves up to become split end.

THE I SLOT

A common adjustment of the I Formation is the I Slot. The flankerback becomes a split end and the tight end drops back into a wingback position about 1½ yards outside the offensive tackle and 1 yard deep in the backfield.

This formation has all backs in position to handle the ball on running plays, which adds tremendously to the number of offensive variations available. It also gives great deception on reverse plays, since the wingback can get the ball quickly after the quarterback has faked to the fullback or tailback.

THE POWER-I

Another variation of the I Formation is the Power-I,

Diagram 19. The Power-I. The flankerback moves in to become halfback.

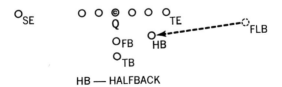

HB — HALFBACK

79

which is usually used in short yardage situations and when a team is close to its opponent's goal line. It can be played with two tight ends or with one end split. The quarterback, fullback and tailback are in the regular I position. The flankerback takes his position as a regular halfback, lined up about 3½ yards deep behind his own offensive tackle.

This formation has great power and great deception, since both the fullback and the wingback can lead to block on inside running plays. Any one of the three backs may end up with the ball after the quarterback has faked to one or two teammates.

THE T FORMATION

The basic T Formation is essentially another variation of the Power-I. The tailback moves to the halfback position, which puts him at the same depth as the fullback and the other halfback. The formation has perfect balance to both sides, can quickly hit every inside spot along the line of scrimmage and has great deception, since any of the three backs may get the ball. This is not a strong passing formation because no receivers are detached wide.

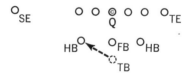

Diagram 20. The T Formation

THE WISHBONE-T FORMATION

The most exciting new development in offensive football is the Wishbone-T attack, pioneered by the University of Texas and adopted by an increasing number of teams including the University of Oklahoma. Teams using this pattern of offense have decisively broken all intercollegiate records in yardage gained and points scored.

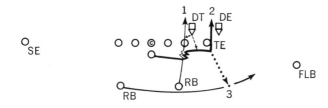

DT — DEFENSIVE TACKLE   DE — DEFENSIVE END

Diagram 21. The Triple Option in Action

The development of the Wishbone is an interesting example of the progress of offensive thinking. Bill Yeoman, coach of the University of Houston team, pioneered the so-called "Triple Option"—a variation of the Open Set —using two wide receivers. See Diagram 21. The running backs are lined up shading the outside of the offensive guards. As the Triple Option begins, one of the running backs hits over his offensive tackle, and the quarterback places the ball on his far hip as he reads the defensive tackle. If the defensive tackle crosses the line of scrimmage, he lets the running back have the ball. If the defensive tackle closes to stop the running back, the quarterback keeps the ball and moves out to option the defensive end (see page 65).

The Wishbone utilizes only one split end, the other wide receiver being moved in to become the fullback positioned about 3½ yards behind the line of scrimmage directly behind the quarterback. See Diagram 22. As the play begins, the

Diagram 22. The Wishbone-T Formation. A one-man change from the Triple Option forms the Wishbone: The flankerback moves in to become fullback.

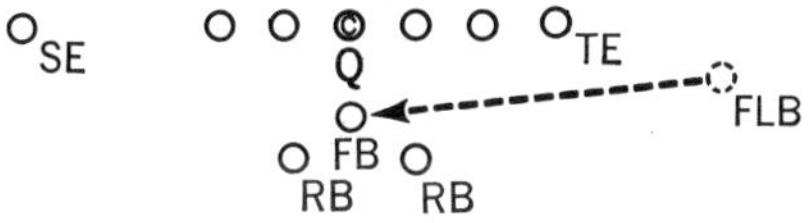

fullback runs over the offensive tackle to the side of the play. The quarterback reads the defensive tackle. If he crosses the line, the quarterback gives the ball to his fullback. But if the defensive tackle stays on the line to play the fullback, the quarterback keeps the ball and moves out to option the defensive end. See Diagram 23.

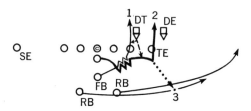

Diagram 23. Triple Option from the Wishbone-T

Both the Wishbone and the Triple Option are devastatingly effective because anything the defense does will be wrong. Since the Wishbone is perfectly balanced, and since the Triple Option can be run either way with equal effectiveness, the defense has no way of knowing the point of attack. In addition, the split end, who is a wide receiver, is usually covered by only one man, which makes it relatively easy for him to get open on pass plays.

BASIC OFFENSIVE THEORY

Defensive football has become increasingly sophisticated and complex. Teams use a variety of defensive alignments. They change the angle of charge and stunt many different ways from each defensive set. The defensive quarterback is trying to outguess the offensive quarterback on every play. This has necessitated development of new offensive tactics. Ascertaining the alignment of the defensive team prior to the snap is helpful. But since the defense will use a variety of charges and patterns from any alignment, the offensive team must be able to read these movements and *adjust the point of attack after the ball is snapped.*

Both the Houston Triple Option and the Wishbone-T attack utilize this principle to perfection. When the ball is snapped, the offense does not know whether it will be given to the faking back, kept by the quarterback or pitched to the trailing halfback. The other plays used—the counter, the counter option and various play-action passes—all start exactly like the Triple Option. Consequently, there is no key available to the defense to give them a quick tip as to the point of attack.

This same principle is essential in developing a sound passing game. Teams that base their offense on the forward pass must teach their quarterback to read whatever coverage is being used and to throw to the second or third receiver when the primary receiver is covered.

9

Team Fundamentals

THE most important team fundamental is proper execution of the starting count. All of the players must break at the same time to beat their opponents to the punch. Here is an effective drill that takes little time and energy but develops the team's skill:

Starting Count Drill. The players hold their hands about 9 inches apart while the quarterback gives the starting count, says, "Break," and then calls the snap signal. At the signal the players clap instead of charging. Scattered claps mean that they are not responding in unison—there should be only one clapping sound. The count should be practiced until it is perfectly executed.

WHAT NOT TO DO

All players must be disciplined to look straight ahead. Leaning by any offensive man will tip off the direction of the play. Looking at the point of attack can also be a give-away. Figures 32, 33, 34 and 35 illustrate some tip-offs.

Another fundamental of offense is not to make errors. A consistently successful offensive team must not fumble, throw interceptions, incur penalties or miss assignments. All of these errors can be avoided by a sound, sensible approach to planning the offense.

Figure 32. Body weight forward is a tip-off that the man will charge straight ahead.

Figure 33. Body weight back is a tip-off that the man will pull out or drop back to protect the passer.

Figure 34. The player who leans and looks
to his right tips off the direction of play.

Figure 35. The player who leans and looks
to his left also tips off the defense.

The common mistake is to have more plays than are needed. A well-balanced offense can be developed which totals only sixteen to eighteen plays.

Actually, the offense needs to attack only four ways: run inside, run outside, reverse to misguide the defense and throw the ball. The passing attack should include drop-back passes, running passes and play-action passes.

It is also a mistake to have plays that are beyond the capabilities of the players. At the University of Oklahoma when we had Tommy McDonald as our left halfback, the running pass was our best play. The season after Tommy graduated, we could not use the play because we did not have a running back who could throw well enough to make it effective.

To sum up: The offense can reduce the incidence of errors by having a limited number of plays that are within the team's physical ability to execute consistently well.

10
Quarterback Strategy

SENSIBLE play selection is essential if the offense is to maintain possession of the ball. A basic rule in quarterback strategy is: *Never try to force the issue with the defense.* In other words, hit its weakest area.

Vertical field position—the position of the ball relative to the defensive team's goal line—should always be a major consideration in play selection. Most coaches divide the field into four zones, as shown in Diagram 24.

Diagram 24. Quarterback's Field Plan

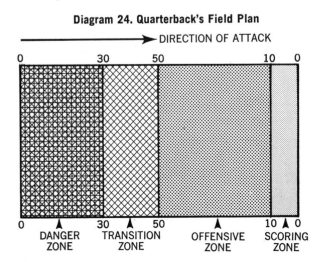

In the danger zone it is absolutely essential to avoid a turnover through a fumble or an interception. This limits the number of offensive plays available to the quarterback. Don't gamble on any play that involves a high risk of a fumble or a pass interception, both of which are almost certain to result in either a field goal or a touchdown by the opponent.

In the transition zone the quarterback can be freer in the use of his total offense, but he still should not gamble with plays that have a high incidence of turnover.

In the offensive zone the quarterback can freely use his entire attack. He can gamble to make a first down to keep possession of the ball.

In the scoring zone the quarterback knows that he has four plays in which to score. He should plan all four before calling the first one. On first and second down, avoid calling plays that might result in any loss of yardage. On later downs, depending on the yards needed to score, go with plays that have the potential for longer gains.

When in the danger, transition and offensive zones, the quarterback's first mission should be: *Make a first down.* This statement sounds obvious and simple, but it isn't. If the quarterback hopes to score on one particular play—a long pass, for example—and isn't successful, the play has been wasted. However, if he thinks in terms of making a first down and is repeatedly successful, it follows that he will eventually score. In addition, he will have maintained possession of the ball—and the team that maintains possession of the ball longest almost always wins.

The quarterback must thoroughly understand that, until his team has possession of the ball deep in the opponent's territory, he has only *three* downs available to him, since he must punt on the fourth down. Whether the advantage stays with the offense or goes to the defense depends on the average gain the offense must make to earn a first down. By averaging 3⅓ yards a play, a steady succession of first downs can be made. Although it is quite simple to make 4 yards on a play, it is difficult to make more than 6 yards.

For example, on "first and 10" the offense is relatively sure that it can make the first down if it does not lose yardage on badly executed plays or throw incomplete passes. A first-down incomplete pass is not particularly damaging to the offense: only 5 yards per play are needed on the two succeeding downs to earn the first down. However, a 5-yard loss on first down means that the offense must average 7½ yards on the two succeeding downs to earn the first down. This is extremely difficult to do against a competent defense.

Except for scouting reports, the quarterback is pretty much in the dark the first time the offense has the ball. He knows the strengths of his own team and has some idea of the weaknesses of the defensive players as individuals, but, until the game begins, it's difficult for him to have a good feel of how things will go.

On first possession, the quarterback is seeking a play that will work. When he finds one that makes 5 yards or more, he has established the basis of his attack. The defensive weakness must be continually exploited, and he should repeat the successful play until the defense makes an adjustment to stop it. Actually, the quarterback should try to anticipate such an adjustment in time to avoid wasting a play. This ability to anticipate and change the play *before* the defense can stop it marks the difference between the great field general and the average signal caller. There is probably no better model for this than Johnny Unitas.

It is axiomatic, but still basic, that the quarterback should call a play the defense doesn't expect. The following list provides the basis of doing this:

- If the defense expects an inside play, run wide.
- If the defense expects a wide play, run inside.
- If the defense expects a pass, run.

93

- If the defense expects a run, pass.
- If direct plays are not successful, use misdirection plays.

One can refine these statements into two fundamental rules of quarterbacking:

(1). The longer the yardage needed, the deeper the linebackers and secondary will play, making it easier to make substantial yardage inside.

(2). The shorter the yardage needed, the tighter the linebackers and secondary will play, making it easier to gain substantial yardage running wide or throwing.

As emphasized before, all eleven players must work together to make a team move consistently well. Only continual practice will develop the required excellence. Work on stance, timing, breaking together and, above all, finding your target and hitting it. Good blocking, ball carrying, passing, receiving and sound quarterbacking, executed by a disciplined, highly motivated team, will result in a winning offense.